Ready to Read
Syllables and Sentences

I like to read.

How to Play

1. Press the Power button to turn the SD-X Reader on or off. The LED will light up when the SD-X Reader is on.

2. Touch the volume buttons found on this page to adjust the volume.

3. Touch words and pictures on the page to hear audio. The monkey gives instructions and starts activities.

4. After two minutes of inactivity, the SD-X Reader will beep and go to sleep.

5. If the batteries are low, the SD-X Reader will beep twice and the LED will start blinking. Replace the batteries by following the instructions on the next page. The SD-X Reader uses two AAA batteries.

6. To use headphones or earbuds, plug them into the headphone jack on the SD-X Reader.

Volume

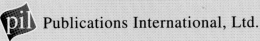 Publications International, Ltd.

Battery Information

Includes two replaceable AAA batteries (UM-4 or LR03).

Battery Installation

1. Open battery door with small flat-head or Phillips screwdriver.
2. Install new batteries according to +/- polarity. If batteries are not installed properly, the device will not function.
3. Replace battery door; secure with small screw.

Battery Safety

Batteries must be replaced by adults only. Properly dispose of used batteries. See battery manufacturer for disposal recommendations. Do not mix alkaline, standard (carbon-zinc), or rechargeable (nickel-cadmium) batteries. Do not mix old and new batteries. Only recommended batteries of the same or equivalent type should be used. Remove weakened or dead batteries. Never short-circuit the supply terminals. Non-rechargeable batteries are not to be recharged. Do not use rechargeable batteries. If batteries are swallowed, in the USA, promptly see a doctor and have the doctor phone 1-202-625-3333 collect. In other countries, have the doctor call your local poison control center. This product uses 2 AAA batteries (2 X 1.5V = 3.0 V). Use batteries of the same or equivalent type as recommended. The supply terminals are not to be short-circuited. Batteries should be changed when sounds mix, distort, or become otherwise unintelligible as batteries weaken. The electrostatic discharge may interfere with the sound module. If this occurs, please simply restart the sound module by pressing any key.

In Europe, the dustbin symbol indicates that batteries, rechargeable batteries, button cells, battery packs, and similar materials must not be discarded in household waste. Batteries containing hazardous substances are harmful to the environment and to health. Please help to protect the environment from health risks by telling your children to dispose of batteries properly and by taking batteries to local collection points. Batteries handled in this manner are safely recycled.

Warning: Changes or modifications to this unit not expressly approved by the party responsible for compliance could void the user's authority to operate the equipment.

NOTE: This equipment has been tested and found to comply with the limits for a Class B digital device, pursuant to Part 15 of the FCC Rules. These limits are designed to provide reasonable protection against harmful interference in a residential installation. This equipment generates, uses, and can radiate radio frequency energy and, if not installed and used in accordance with the instructions, may cause harmful interference to radio communications. However, there is no guarantee that interference will not occur in a particular installation. If this equipment does cause harmful interference to radio or television reception, which can be determined by turning the equipment off and on, the user is encouraged to try to correct the interference by one or more of the following measures: Reorient or relocate the receiving antenna. Increase the separation between the equipment and receiver. Connect the equipment into an outlet on a circuit different from that to which the receiver is connected. Consult the dealer or an experienced radio TV technician for help.

Contributing writers: Natalie Goldstein, Michele Warrence-Schreiber

Consultant: Elizabeth C. Stull, Ph.D.

Illustrators: George Ulrich, James Schlottman

Picture Credits: Art Explosion; Comstock RF; Corbis RF; Image Club Graphics; PhotoDisc; PIL Collection; StockByte

Louis Weber, C.E.O., Publications International, Ltd.

7373 North Cicero Avenue   Ground Floor, 59 Gloucester Place
Lincolnwood, Illinois 60712   London W1U 8JJ

Customer Service:

1-888-724-0144 or customer_service@pilbooks.com
www.pilbooks.com

SD-X Interactive is a registered trademark in the United States and Canada.

Manufactured in China.

8 7 6 5 4 3 2 1
ISBN-10: 1-4508-2061-1
ISBN-13: 978-1-4508-2061-5

Keep On Track!

Mon-key! Mon-key has two word parts or **syllables**.

How Many Syllables?

Use syllables.

wagon

ball

apple

kite

elephant

What Is It?

Nouns name a person, place, or thing.
A **singular** noun stands for one thing.

tree

cat

cup

desk

sun

A Day Trip

Some nouns are the names of places.
School and **home** are nouns for places.

lake   store

home   park

We left _____.

We went to the _____.

We went to the _____.

We went to the _____.

Then we came back _____.

 **We had fun!**

What's My Name?

The name of a person or place is a **proper noun**. A proper noun always begins with a capital letter.

Pam Smith	Main Street
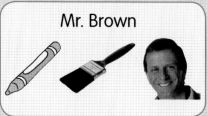	

Mr. Brown	Bob
	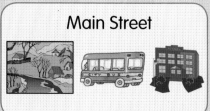

my pet Fluffy	Elton School

Two Together

Some big words are made of two small words. The new word is called a **compound word**.

bird + cage = birdcage

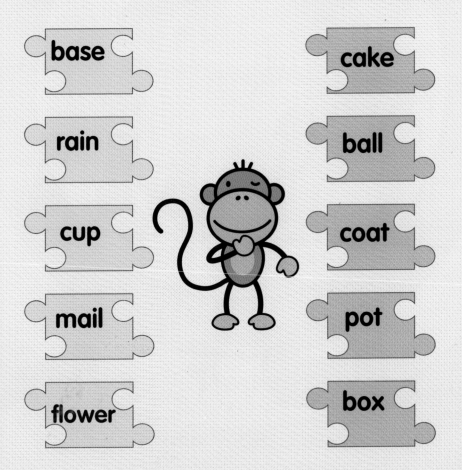

base

cake

rain

ball

cup

coat

mail

pot

flower

box

More Than One

Plural nouns

Some nouns stand for more than one thing. These are **plural nouns**. Many plural nouns get an **s** at the end.

one cat   two cats

pet dog dogs   socks foot sock

apple apples red   pigs pig piggy

More Than One–Again

Nouns that end in **s**, **sh**, **ch**, **x**, or **z** get **es** at the end to show more than one.

dish dish**es** | fox fox**es**

glass___

whale___

peach___

box___

es

s

I Can Do It!

Action words tell what people and things do. They are called **verbs**.

Some verbs are

dance | **walk**

I can

run
girl
fast

I can

boy
sing
hair

I can

write
pen
book

I can

water
lake
swim

I Can Do It Again!

 The baby sleeps.

 The boy reads the book.

 He plays basketball.

 The bird sings in a tree.

 We bake cookies.

What Did You Do?

Past-tense verbs tell what you did in the past. Most past-tense verbs end with **d** or **ed**.

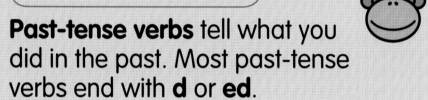

 The boy _____ basketball.

(**played**) (**jump**) (**play**)

 The boy _____ of candy.

(**sleep**) (**dreamed**) (**dream**)

 The baby _____ the ball.

(**roll**) (**rolled**) (**round**)

 The girl _____ a picture.

(**painted**) (**paint**) (**brush**)

What Else Did You Do?

Some past-tense verbs
do not end with **d** or **ed**.

Present Tense	Past Tense
go	went
eat	ate
give	gave
tell	told
run	ran

Jim _____ to the beach.

went	go

Billy _____ an apple.

eat	ate

Jill _____ her friend
a present.

give	gave

To Be or Not To Be?

The verb **to be** is different from other verbs.

Present tense of **to be**	Past tense of **to be**
I **am** happy.	I **was** happy.
He **is** happy.	He **was** happy.
Pam **is** happy.	Pam **was** happy.
It **is** sunny.	It **was** sunny.
You **are** nice.	You **were** nice.
We **are** friends.	We **were** friends.
They **are** happy.	They **were** happy.

Present Tense of To Be

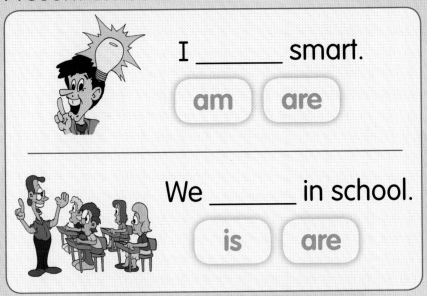

I _____ smart.

am   are

We _____ in school.

is   are

Past Tense of To Be

I _____ cold.

was   are

You _____ asleep.

am   were

Pronoun Practice

A **pronoun** is a word that stands for a noun.

The **cup** is full.	**It** is full.
The **girl** is happy.	**She** is happy.
The **boy** has fun.	**He** has fun.
Emma is my friend.	**You** are my friend.
Bob and I like pizza.	**We** like pizza.
Liz and Pam play.	**They** play.

it   she   he   they

Let's Agree

A noun or pronoun must match a verb.

I talk.   You talk.
You talk.   We talk.
She talks.   They talk.
He talks.

I _____ to run.

like   likes

The kids _____ ball.

plays   play

She _____ rope.

jumps   jump

No, No, No

Some words mean no. These words are called **negative** words.

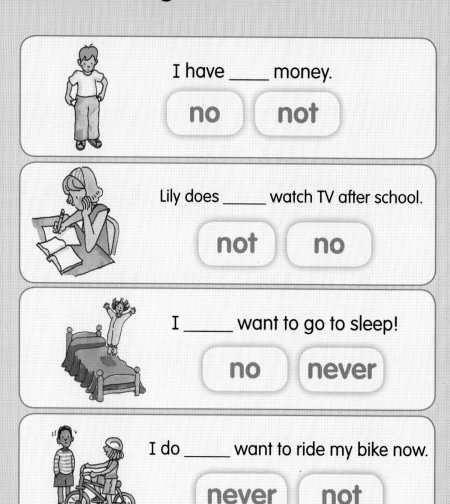

I have _____ money.

no   **not**

Lily does _____ watch TV after school.

not   **no**

I _____ want to go to sleep!

no   **never**

I do _____ want to ride my bike now.

never   **not**

Shorties

An elephant **isn't** small.

I'm not hungry.

I **don't** want to go out today.

It's my favorite food.

Sounds the Same

Some words sound the same, but they mean different things.

 son    sun

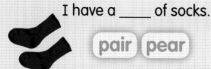

ant   aunt   flower   flour

no   know   pair   pear

I have a ____ of socks.

pair   pear

It is a pretty ____.

flower   flour

The ____ ran across the floor.

aunt   ant

Liz is eating a ____.

pair   pear

I ____ how to read.

no   know

I ____ a bird from my window.

see   sea

Look-Alikes

Some words look the same, but they have different meanings.

the bark of a tree

the bark of a dog

The boy threw the **ball**.

I can hear the school bell **ring**.

A **bat** flies at night.

I write with a **pen**.

Opposites

Some words have opposite meanings. For example, the words **up** and **down** are opposites.

light

dark

short

happy

hot

small

fast

sad

cold

tall

slow

big